To Hawken

M000031580

$\mathcal{D}$Life is a
ance

Who is Going to Lead?

Kae Harper Childs

THE PIER PRESS
Isle of Palms, South Carolina

This book is dedicated to my son Brad, and his wife Mary Ann; my daughter, Harper, and her husband David; and my four precious granddaughters, Addie, Tate, Pressley Ann, and Brooke, with the hope that I have left you with a legacy of joy and love of dance.

Contents

Forward

Life is a Dance Who is Going to Lead? is a wonderful metaphor for life. Kae Harper Childs has perfectly captured the music woven through a believer's life within this collection of devotions.

Kae uses her love of dance and her life experiences to paint a complete picture. Her insights into everyday life help us all to look for God's fingerprints, no matter our circumstances. She encourages, challenges, and most of all, teaches us to recognize God's leading in the intricate dance steps of life.

Her words swing and sway as she reminds us that our partner in life is God. He will never let us go, and holds us tightly to keep us from falls and missteps. But the true beauty of the dance comes when we surrender to His lead, and follow Him.

This is a book to keep on your nightstand and read again and again. I know I will!

Edie Melson, author of *While My Soldier Serves*

Introduction

Going to Folly Beach, South Carolina, with my family every summer created some of my best memories as a child. These trips had a profound impact on my life.

Each July, together with my mother's sister and her family, we would rent a house within walking distance of the beach. The days were filled with sand, sea water, and too much sun. The southern nights were typical for July: hot and humid. We would fall asleep, burned and exhausted, under the oscillating fans with the curtains blowing in the breeze from the open windows.

But the best part of each Folly Beach stay was the dancing. Every evening after dinner, we would go to the pavilion, listen to the beach music, and watch the couples do the Shag (the South Carolina State Dance). As a result, my dreams as a little girl weren't focused on getting married and having children like other girls I knew. Instead, my dream was to one day be dancing with good-looking guys on the pier.

In my lifetime, I've held the hands of hundreds of men and women and taught them to dance. I've also been blessed to hold the hands of my children and grandchildren through the years. But, looking back, I can see how God used dance as a theme to choreograph the steps of my life. I've held tightly to His hand and let Him lead me. I can say without a doubt, the most important hand I have held throughout my life is that of my heavenly Father.

I share many of my life experiences in the pages of this book. Through these experiences I have learned that trying to take the lead of your daily life away from the hands it should be in may get you through, but it will never create the best life you can live. My prayer for you as you read my words is that you find laughter, love, and joy, in these pages. Mostly, I hope you will decide to hold the hand of our Father everyday of your life.

All Eyes on Me

Many are the plans in a man's heart, but it is the
Lord's purpose that prevails.
John 10:27

All eyes are on me, and I'm standing in front of eighty ladies wearing their pearls and heels in a southern country club. They've turned their chairs around, pushed away their luncheon plates, and they're patiently waiting to hear what I have to say. The musician has finished her song and has taken her seat among them. It's my turn. I'm hoping my voice won't crack from nervousness and that my knees don't buckle.

Many years ago I was introduced to Stonecroft Ministries, an interdenominational organization that sponsors ladies' luncheons and Bible studies along with other outreach programs. The purpose of these meetings is to introduce Jesus to people of all walks of life and to teach us how to follow His plans for our lives. Now I find myself at one of these luncheons and, for the first time, I am the speaker.

Looking back on my life, I can see how God weaves my life together by allowing me to use all of my experiences – both good and bad – to share with others. As a dance instructor for many years I've learned, and continue to learn more everyday, how His loving arms lead me. It's fitting that the title of my talk today is *Life Is a Dance Who Is Going to Lead?* It's a perfect example of my experiences placed in God's hands. As He leads me to share with others, He must be the leader and we must follow His lead.

After much laughter and many tears, before I know it, I'm at the door receiving a hug from each lady as she leaves. So many thank me for sharing my words and experiences. Many say I've been an inspiration to them and they could relate to what I said.

My voice was strong and my knees didn't buckle. My loving leader, Jesus, has lead me once again through another experience. This time it was helping others to see that He is our perfect leader in the dance of life.

Lord, help us to be good followers of You.

Kae's first speaking engagement.

A Piece of My Father

Have we not all one father?
Malachi 2:10

There were times growing up as one of four girls when I felt time alone with my father was scarce. Everyone seemed to want his attention, and his daughters were no different. Our one father was split into so many pieces between work and his family there was never enough of him to go around.

I don't ever remember Daddy telling me he loved me. Dancing with him was the time when I felt loved by him and knew I was special to him. On some occasions the four of us girls would put on a record in our living room and practice dancing with our father. I can go back into that moment in time in my mind now as if it were yesterday. Daddy was a very nice looking man and a great dancer. Whenever he took me in his arms to dance, I was in heaven. I had his full attention. He would look at me and say, "All right, Honey, it's your turn." I hated that the dance always ended too soon.

Here on earth, it is sometimes hard, but many children must share their fathers, or some don't even have a father. However, someday we all will have endless time with our heavenly Father. I don't know how He'll work that out, but I know He will. And until that time comes, we can have time alone with Him every day, all day long. Once we ask Him to enter our heart, He is always with us.

And, yes, we do ALL have one father, our Father in Heaven.

Kae's Mother and Daddy

A Special Friend

A friend loveth at all times.
Proverbs 17:17

At the beginning of the seventh grade, my family moved to Greenville. That was only thirty miles away from where we were living, but it may as well have been a million miles. I remember how hard it was to leave my friends of twelve years. We were too young to drive, and we couldn't make unlimited long distance calls like the teenagers today, so we really had no way of keeping in touch. Initially, I was very lonely.

Soon after we moved, a girl named Gayle and I began to "hit it off." We lived on opposite sides of town, but before long, we started spending the night together. One thing we had in common was that we both loved to dance. We'd spend hours and hours making up dance moves. Growing up, I had to share a room with my younger sister. Because of that,

I didn't like to invite friends to sleep over at my house. It worked out great for us that Gayle had only one brother and her own room, and that she wanted me to stay over as much as possible.

We stayed close as we got older. When we got into high school, she got a new, bright-red convertible. Boy, did we think we were something riding around town in that! I remember one night we snuck out of the house and spent most of the night just sitting in the car in the drive way, (we knew better than to actually move it) listening to the radio, talking, and laughing. That seems like yesterday although it's been fifty years!

Gayle was one of the few girls in our graduating class to leave South Carolina to go to college. She went to the University of Miami. After graduation, she married a boy named Tony and they lived together in Florida. Not too long into their marriage she was diagnosed with Multiple Sclerosis. She slowly lost all use of every part of her body except her left arm. She had just enough strength and coordination to hold a telephone. She and I talked frequently, and I went to stay with her as often as possible. We both knew how fortunate she was to have Tony to take care of her.

Suddenly, and much to our surprise, Tony dropped dead of a heart attack leaving Gayle totally helpless. During this time, Gayle still sounded exactly like herself. Nothing had changed. She always wanted to know about how my dance classes were going. And never did I sense a feeling of "poor me," even though I was the one out dancing almost every night and she could only use one hand. She never acted like she was bitter or mad even though she had every reason to be. In fact, I remember asking her one time while we were reminiscing about our dance moves, "Can you believe that I'm actually getting paid to teach those dances?"

To that she said, "It doesn't surprise me at all. I always knew you would."

Recently, I got a call from Gayle's brother. He called to tell me she had died from complications of M.S. Through my tears, all I could think of was how blessed I was to have had such a true friend. But the truest friend of all is the friend we have in Jesus. God has given Jesus to us to teach us how to love one another and how to be a good friend to the people he puts in our lives. Gayle demonstrated Jesus' love all her life and for that I am truly grateful.

He Will Never Leave Nor Forsake You

Dear brothers and sisters, when troubles of any kind
come your way, consider it an opportunity for great joy.
For you know that when your faith is tested,
your endurance has a chance to grow.
James 1:2-3

After fifteen years of marriage, Don, my childhood sweetheart and dance partner, told me he didn't love me anymore. He was leaving the children and me for another woman. I was devastated. We sold our beautiful new home and went our separate ways.

Over the summer we were separated, I lived in Hilton Head and taught dancing part time while he stayed in Greenwood. The children went back and forth between our homes while they were out of school. At the end of summer, I went back to Greenwood so that Brad and Harper could start the new school year. I continued teaching dance in Hilton Head and commuted back and forth a few days a week. It was during this time, a man came into my life who made me forget the pain of Don's decision. I felt like I was in love again. But my children's sadness because we were not living together as a family continued to weigh on me.

After a full year, the day before our divorce was to be final, Don called to ask if he could come over to talk. I agreed, but I really had nothing to say to him. I was in love with someone else and had already moved on. He told me that he had made a huge mistake and wanted the children and me back in his life. Even though I didn't trust him yet, I also wanted our family back together again, so I agreed to a six month trial dating period.

At the end of the six months, we were happier than ever. Don had done all the things he had promised to do and my trust in him was re-established. In celebration of our new life together, we renewed our vows. It was at this point that we decided leaving Greenwood was the best decision for our marriage and our family. We left town and started all over.

That was twenty years ago now and our love for each other is still clear in my mind. Even though Don is now gone, whenever I think about him, I imagine that we are smiling at each other while he is holding me in his arms moving around the dance floor.

I'm so thankful that I have a Savior who is always smiling at me and holding me throughout the day and night. Looking back, I can see the supernatural desire God had placed in my heart to have our family back together. It allowed time for my love for him to be rekindled. I have no doubt that one day, Don and I will be dancing together again in Heaven.

Don, Kae, and family, at their vow renewal ceremony.

My Mourning into Dancing

Thou hast turned my mourning into dancing.
Psalm 30:11

"The doctors think I have kidney cancer," Don, my husband of twenty-five years, said to me.

Sure enough after several tests, it was confirmed he did have kidney cancer. We couldn't believe our ears. Almost immediately he had surgery to have his left kidney removed and was assured that he was going to be healthy again. Two years later, the cancer metastasized and, after three years and a hard fought battle, he died at the age of fifty-three. Even though the children and I had a strong faith in God and a belief in Heaven, it was a devastating blow. Soon after he passed away, both children left for college and I was alone, feeling very much the empty nester. It was a huge challenge for me.

My good friends watched me struggling and began insisting I go out with them. Dancing was their major form of entertainment. I hadn't been dancing in quite a while. During the five years of Don's illness, I wasn't able to dance as much as I had done in the past. I'm so glad my friends cared enough to give me the extra push I needed.

That was when I began teaching dance classes every week, and it has brought me some my greatest joys in life. Doing something for others and making them happy is so fulfilling. God has truly turned my mourning into dancing. He can do the same for you.

Maybe you have a friend who could use your encouragement today.

Don laughing.

Happy Birthday, Cha, Cha, Cha!

From them will come songs of thanksgiving
and the sound of rejoicing...
Jeremiah 30:19

My daughter, Harper, and her husband, David, have two girls – Addison and Tate. My son, Brad, and his wife, Mary Ann, also have two daughters – Pressley Ann and Brooke.

Since both families are extremely busy with work, school, sports, piano, etc., we have to work really hard to get us all together. Planning at Christmas is no different. We know that celebrating the true meaning of Christmas sometimes gets lost with all the gifts and parties going on around us.

One Christmas, when my granddaughters were little, I was especially moved by and proud of my family. After much coordination, we sat down together and took up one entire pew at the Christmas Eve service at Brad's church. We had finally moved past the "wiggly" stage with the girls and could thoroughly enjoy listening to the service and take it all in. It was short and sweet with lots of Christmas music and touching stories of Christmas miracles. The service ended with each person lighting a candle. I breathed a sigh of relief when, after the prayer, we blew out the candles and all of the girls' pretty long curls were still there.

We spoke to and hugged several families on our way out. The cold December air, mixed with light rain, hit us in the face as we hurried to our cars. We were so happy to be together on Christmas Eve, and knowing that Santa was coming later that night made the girls giddy with excitement.

Brad's house was decorated to the hilt. Twinkling lights greeted us as we pulled up, and we ran in to get out of the cold and enjoy Christmas Eve dinner.

The dinner table was set. A delicious feast of turkey, dressing, cranberry sauce, casseroles, and hot rolls were put in big bowls and platters on the table. Before we began, we grabbed the hand of the person next to us and let the little girls sing grace:

God, our Father, God, our Father
We thank you, We thank you
For our many blessings, For our many blessings
Amen, Amen

As soon as they finished singing, Tate (who was 10 at the time) asked, "Can I say another blessing?"

"Of course," the adults responded in unison.

Tate bowed her head and said the most touching prayer and ended it with "Thank you, God, for giving us Jesus and Happy Birthday."

Through watery eyes, we all dug into our scrumptious meal! We had barely finished when the girls cried out for dessert. In addition to a side table of specially prepared sweets consisting of pies, cookies, and candy, there was a birthday cake.

"Let's sing Happy Birthday to Jesus!" Brooke, our six year old, exclaimed.

"OK, get the candles," Mary Ann said.

With the glow of the candles on our faces, young and old alike sang Happy Birthday to Jesus. At the end, Addison and Tate – like they would have done at the end of any other friend or family member's birthday song – shouted out a loud "Cha, cha, cha!" The table broke out in laugher!

At this moment, my mind flashed to a picture of Jesus laughing that both Harper and I have had hanging in our kitchens for years. It seemed He was truly laughing with us right at that moment as we sang His birthday song: Happy Birthday, Jesus, Cha, Cha, Cha!

The Bible says "He wept," and I feel sure He must have also laughed!

Kae and family at Christmas.

When Life Gives You Lemons

I am glad and rejoice with all of you.
Philippians 2:17

I was invited to do a "spot light dance" at a Shag Extravaganza put on by the Capital City Shag Club one weekend in Columbia. There were four hundred and fifty people at this event, mostly over the age of forty, who were all expecting to have a wonderful time. Hard working committees had planned the entertainment months in advance and had the ballroom decked out in a gorgeous black and white theme. Fun gift bags were at each place setting and flowers and balloons decorated each table.

Rita and her husband, Henry, were active members in the Capital City Shag Club. Recently she had been diagnosed with ALS. Sadly, she had quickly gone from teaching Shag several times a week to being wheel-chair-bound. But that didn't stop her from participating in the opening act which featured twenty beautiful ladies all dressed in black pants, starched white dress shirts, and bright red cummerbunds. They were doing a Radio City Music Hall Rockettes rendition.

Rita came out, pushed by her proud husband, and led the other ladies as they high-stepped across the floor. Her smile was enough to bring tears of joy and compassion to the eyes of each person who witnessed it. All of the ladies did a wonderful job that night, but I'll bet if you asked anyone there, the most memorable of all of them for years to come will be Rita.

When life gives you lemons, make lemonade.

Dance like No One is Watching

Then shall the young women rejoice in the dance.
Jeremiah 31:13

Each year in July, boys and girls who are between the ages of six and twenty one are invited to go to North Myrtle Beach to have their own week of Shag. One summer I took Addie, my 13 year old granddaughter, and her best friend, Maxine, to participate for the first time. Five hundred kids came together in the grand ballroom of the beautiful Ocean Drive Golf and Resort Hotel. Before we arrived, I thought Addie would be more tempted to swim in the ocean, as she loves the beach. To my surprise, she just wanted to dance. While the girls had only had a few professional dance lessons, Addie had grown up shagging. (After all, I am a Shag teacher and her mother loves to dance.) Maxine seemed to be picking it up quickly as well after just a few hours of dancing with the group.

One of the highlights of this week each summer is the "shoe give away". Whenever a new girl or boy comes to the Junior S.O.S. (Society of Stranders) week, he or she can pick out a nice, but gently used, pair of dance shoes for their own. The women who help them are extremely helpful. Both Addie and Maxine had a ball selecting their shoes and left the shoe-room dancing.

During the week, all of the assisting adults are volunteers. They are helping the girls and boys to learn to dance and have an all-around good time. They offer ice cream socials, dance lessons, dance contests, and keep the pace moving. Each morning Addie and Maxine would be up and ready to go by ten a.m. and by ten p.m. they were too tired to pick up another foot. I remember saying to Ellen Taylor (the lady who originally came up with the shoe room idea), "The only thing that could be more wonderful than being at North Myrtle Beach shagging yourself is to be watching your grandchildren learn to love it."

One day after the lessons in the ballroom ended and everyone had left to go to lunch, Addie and Maxine wanted to stay behind. They continued to dance even though they both were beginning to get blisters on their feet. I sat in the corner reading over some material while they made up their dance routine. They had legs and arms in the air and big smiles from one to the other, and they ended with a deep bow as if they just performed for a thousand people. I tried not to look but couldn't hold back the smile at how free and innocent they were.

The day came when we had to leave. Addie and Maxine hugged all the adults who had helped throughout the week.

When they approached a really nice man we had seen taking videos all week, he smiled and said, "Aren't you the two girls who were dancing in the ballroom together?

With sheepish smiles they blushed, not realizing that someone had been watching them.

He said, "That was absolutely beautiful! I filmed it and I'd like to put that to music and make a video out of it, if that's all right with you."

They looked at each other and said, "Sure," and skipped off arm in arm, laughing.

In life we should always dance like no one is watching.

Addie with her mom, Harper, her dad, David and sister, Tate.

An Unexpected Assignment

Blessed are those who have learned to acclaim you,
who walk in the light of your presence. Psalm 89:15

As my friend Linda and I walked through the lobby of the Phoenix Inn, we could hear the music of The Drifters singing "Carolina Girls" coming from inside the Magnolia Room. Linda was visiting from out of town, and she was curious about my Shag club's weekly dance night. I think she had visions of a group much different from what she found. So many people do have misconceptions about dancers.

We could hear laughter from the people already enjoying the dance, and I could hardly wait to join them. On our way in, we stopped to say hello to a friend of mine, Ann, who was outside the Magnolia Room talking to her dance partner, Steve. I introduced Linda to them and then asked, "Ann, how is your arm doing?" She had injured it a while prior to that.

"Not very well. I'm so frustrated. I don't know what else I can do," she answered me. "The doctor wants to me to have surgery, but even he seems to be stumped!"

Before I realized it, I heard myself say, "Let's pray about it. Would that be OK with you?"

She said, "Yes, I'd like to."

I took her hand and Linda's. Steve came closer to join our circle. Right there, with the music playing in the next room, we bowed our heads and asked God to give Ann's doctor wisdom and for a full recovery of her arm. Then Linda and I went on to enjoy an evening of shagging.

Sometime later, I ran into Ann again and asked her about her arm. She answered me with the enthusiasm of someone whose worries had been lifted. "It's so much better! I had surgery and I am on my way to a full recovery!" I thanked God for healing my friend and for allowing me have the privilege of praying for her.

Ann's healing reminded me that we never know what God has planned for us in a given day. Linda and I had just planned to enjoy the dance that evening, but God had another, more important assignment for me. I felt privileged to be part of God's plan to heal Ann. That day, I renewed my resolve to ask God to help me be aware of the many chances we have each day to help lead others to Him and His healing powers. Had I been ashamed or too afraid to offer to pray for my friend, I would have missed out on the opportunity to be used in such a big way by Him.

Thank you, Lord, for trusting me with the opportunity to share your love with others.

———— ≈ ————

Kae and her friend Linda on the water.

———— ≈ ————

Strength for the Weary

He gives strength to the weary and increases the power
of the weak....those who hope in the Lord will renew their
strength. They will soar on wings like eagles.
Isaiah 40:29-31

Recently I tripped and fell and I fell hard. My left wrist was broken in three places, and my right knee was fractured. I needed to have surgery to repair the damage I had done to my body and then I would require some recovery time to heal. I was going to be totally dependent on someone to help me. Fortunately, my son and daughter lived nearby.

After my surgery, I hobbled into my daughter's home to begin my recuperation. I was weary and needed rest. It was then I saw the book *Joni*, by Joni Eareckson Tada, lying on a table and I picked it up. The book is the autobiographical story of Joni who, as a young girl, had become paralyzed in a diving accident.

Every night during my recovery I read a few chapters. The more I read about her struggles, the smaller my struggles seemed. The more I read about her faith in God despite her trials, the more my faith in God grew. Even though I had gone through far less than Joni had during my fall, surgery, and recovery, my faith was made stronger through her writing.

I've always had an appreciation for writers, but my appreciation for writers like Joni Eareckson Tada - ones that encourage thousands of people to press on through difficult situations - became even stronger. I know for me, her obedience has strengthened my belief that God is present in whatever I am going through.

My hope is that my words will reach someone during their time of need just as Joni's did for me. As a writer, it's sometimes hard to press on and see beyond the words on the page in front of you. I'm constantly questioning my work. I try to make my writing just right, but I must be reminded I never know how God is going to use my humble words.

He is the Almighty and we must trust Him, and His plans alone.

Waiting for the Storm

*…His way is in the whirlwind and the storm,
and clouds are the dust of his feet."*
Nahum 1:3

Three times each year for the past twenty years, 15,000 men and women have come together to shag dance in North Myrtle Beach. Since the first time I attended about ten years ago, I have only missed it a few times, and that was only because of health issues. Even though all of those thousands of people spend up to ten days at a time together in close quarters, I have never heard a cross word between two people. Everyone comes to have fun.

Just about every time I go, I see a beautiful blonde lady who looks healthy and energetic. She dances most every dance. If I've ever met her, I don't remember, but she always greets me with a smile and says, "Hello."

Last year, when I arrived ready for a fun filled week, I spotted the same pretty lady being pushed in a wheel chair by another lady.

"What has happened?" I wondered to myself.

Later, I found out she had contracted a degenerative muscular disease and could no longer dance like she had in the past. Later that evening, I walked into one of the dance clubs and spotted her in her wheel chair. She was in the middle of the floor being pushed around to the music by a dance partner, and grinning from ear to ear.

"What a wonderful guy to ask her to dance," I thought. "And to push her around the dance floor." He seemed to be having as much fun as she. "What a friend!"

I don't know who that man was, but I liked him immediately. When I got back home, the quote on my refrigerator holds new meaning. It reads "Life isn't about waiting for the storm to pass, it's about learning how to dance in the rain."

Truly that lovely lady is living this quote.

A Southern Tradition

Through love, serve one another.
Galatians 5:13

I had just spent a week at my home on the Isle of Palms and was heading back to Greenville, South Carolina. Passing by Foster's Pub in Mount Pleasant, I decided to stop. It was Sunday night, after all, and this Sunday night was a special one. It was the end of my birthday week. Even though I was running late, I felt my packed car being pulled in Foster's direction.

On Sunday nights at Foster's, Jim Bowers is the "D.J." to about a hundred people who come by to shag, visit with each other, and catch up on the happenings from the week before. Jim (who is about the age of my son), and I, have taught Shag together for many years and I love him dearly. It's a great end to my week when I am able to spend time with him at Foster's.

Surrounded by friends and fun, the evening seemed to fly by. The realization that I had to leave my friends had settled on me. I had a three hour trip ahead of me and it was already 8 o'clock.

But before I left, I had one last request. "Jim, would you play 'Try Mattie' for me?" I asked him.

Jim wasn't at all surprised by my request. He knows how much I like that song and can't resist dancing to it. As the song started, I heard Jim announce to the crowd "It's Kae Childs' birthday weekend! Let's do a birthday dance!"

It was an unexpected surprise for me, even though the birthday dance is a tradition among "shaggers". The men in the crowd lined up to dance with me and one took my hand to start it off. For the next four minutes of the song, I went from one partner to another. As soon as one man had danced a few steps, another hand was reaching out to twirl me away. Some of my partners would shout out over the music, "Happy Birthday, Kae!" and some would whisper "Happy Birthday," in my ear as they twirled me.

Everyone watched and clapped, enjoying the fun of the birthday dance. When it was over, I was giddy with excitement and energy. What a great experience! Even though I had done this many times throughout my shagging years (which date as far back as high school), it's just as exhilarating all these years later.

When the music finished, I gave Jim a hug and thanked him, grabbed my car keys, and said my goodbyes to all my friends. The echo of the "Happy Birthdays" were still ringing in my ears as I pulled away from Foster's and headed out of town.

What a fun way to feel the love and warmth of all my friends. Some of whose names I don't even know, but I've seen them around and I feel like I know them. It sure makes getting another year older a lot easier. I was leaving with a glow-exhausted and happy-tired. My cup was full and running over.

During my three hour drive back to Greenville I found myself thinking about the birthday dance tradition. What a truly unusual tradition the birthday dance among shaggers is. I wish every girl could experience it. I felt loved by my friends and I felt loved by God. It was as if on this night God chose to use this wonderful southern tradition to reach down from Heaven and whisper "Happy Birthday, Kae" in my ear. He truly loves us so.

Kae with DJ Jim Bowers, President of East Cooper Shag Club

God's Perfect Timing

To everything there is a season and a time to every
purpose under the heaven: a time to be born,
a time to die…and a time to dance.
Ecclesiastes 3:1-4

We can plan things, wish for things, and work for things to happen for years, but only God knows when some things will happen, and we must accept that.

I am a dance teacher and have been for many years. I started teaching Slimnastics, which is exercising to music, then moved to teaching line dancing, which began with the John Travolta's *Saturday Night Fever*. Later, I taught ballroom dancing like the Disco and the Cha-Cha. Finally, I settled into the Shag, the South Carolina State Dance.

The Shag is much like the Jitterbug. A man and woman hold one hand and make steps to a specific count. Most teachers use the count: one and two, three and four, five, six. The timing of these numbers for the footwork must go with the beat of the drum in the music. If a student learns the footwork but doesn't understand the timing, the dance doesn't look the way it's meant to. The teacher focuses on correct timing so the end result will be a beautiful dance.

Recently, Keith, a friend of mine, passed away. Everyone expected his wife Jane to die first, since she had battled cancer for years and had barely avoided death several times. It was during one of her remissions when Keith was unexpectedly diagnosed with cancer himself, and quickly passed away leaving Jane behind. We were all surprised at that turn of events.

We never know why and often, we don't understand God's timing. Dance students learn to trust their teacher to connect the timing and the music to create a beautiful dance. As God's children, we trust Him to connect the steps of our lives to His timing to create a beautiful life for us. He is in control and wants our very best.

Thank You

Let the message of Christ dwell among you richly...
singing to God with gratitude in your hearts.

I happened to be watching as one of my Shag students at the University of South Carolina finished the dance with his assigned partner. He held her hands in his, looked into her eyes and said, "Thank you."

I couldn't help but smile. "That was nice, Holland," I complimented him.

One of the first things I teach all of my students, whether it's a private lesson or a college course, is to say, "Thank you" after you've danced. Holland gave his partner the gift of gratitude to thank her for her gift dancing with him.

Who doesn't like to be thanked? We all love to be appreciated. Expressing gratitude is a way we can show love to God and to others. Being thankful for everything is a good habit that we can strive to cultivate. An easy way to start is to wake up each morning and thank God for the new day He has given us. We can thank Him for a good night's sleep, for a warm bed, for eyes to see, and ears to hear. I find that the more things I take the time to thank Him for, the more my eyes are opened to the blessings – both big and small – in my life. And the more blessings I recognize, the more my life becomes filled with joy.

Being thankful for the gifts in my life is, in itself, a gift.

Kae dancing with JoJo Putnam, legendary shagger.

*Jeremy Webb, National Jr. Shag Champion,
demonstrating with Kae for USC class*

Please, No More Turns!

*You will show me the path of life; in your
presence is fullness of joy; at your right hand
are pleasures forevermore.*
Psalm 16:11

Turns are a big part of most every kind of dance. A ballerina, I understand, has to keep her eyes on a certain spot to keep her balance. There are times I will get a Shag partner who continues turning me around and around. Sometimes I have to ask him to stop, because I get so dizzy I think I might fall.

One morning, while I was sitting in my bed spending time with the Lord, I was distracted by an internal debate about how to spend my day.

Do I drive to Ocean Drive for the last weekend of SOS, the coming together of thousands to Shag?

Do I drive to my home in Charleston to spend the night there to and be my home church in the morning?

Do I stay here in Greenville and do special things with my granddaughters?

All of my choices sounded good but which one would be the best use of my time? It was making me as dizzy as too many turns on the dance floor. I knew I needed direction and I needed it fast!

The Bible tells us to keep our eyes on Christ and He will direct our every move. As I got down on my knees by my bed that morning to pray, I remembered a verse that helped me make my decision. Hebrews 12:2 reads, "Let us direct our eyes on Jesus, the author and perfecter of our faith." It was as if the right answer was illuminated after I put my focus in the right place.

Thank you, Lord, for the Bible and all its wisdom.

Kae and dancing partner.

Line Dancing

Let all that you do be done in love.
1 Corinthians 16:14

A line dance is when people line up on the dance floor in one line. Then, if there are many dancers, more lines are formed. There may be only three or four people, or up to hundreds at a time. The best thing about line dancing is that you don't have to have a partner to do it.

The first line dance that comes to my mind became popular in the fifties and was made famous by the movie *Shag*. It's called "The Continental." The next line dance I recall was taken from the movie *Saturday Night Fever* with John Travolta.

The release of that movie coincided with the time I began teaching dance for the first time. I was living in Greenwood, South Carolina, and fell in love with it. (And John Travolta wasn't bad, either!) I was already teaching an exercise class called "Slimnastics," so I added the line dance taken from the movie to my classes. The ladies loved it.

Line dancing is so popular now, you can hardly go out dancing without a line dance breaking out, and most parties and wedding receptions will play "The Electric Slide." It's the most recognizable line dance in recent years. People of all ages can enjoy it. One of the best things about line dancing is if you make a mistake, it really doesn't matter, you just grin and keep going.

Over the years, I've expanded the places I teach line dancing. One of the places I've taught for the last five years is at church. The women in this "ladies only" class have become so close and our relationships have extended beyond the class. We've had the pleasure of taking our music and moves to a nursing home to share with the residents.

What a joy teaching line dancing has been for me. It's all about having a good time and its wonderful exercise. If you haven't had the chance to try it, next time you see a line dance breakout, just step up in the middle of the group and give it a try.

Carolina Girl

…It is more blessed to give than to receive.
Acts 20:35

I was awakened by a phone call at 8 o'clock one morning.

"Good morning, Miss Kae. This is Gena from the Palmetto Nursing Home. You have been recommended to me to teach the Shag to our residents. Would you be interested?"

I have been teaching the Shag, the South Carolina State Dance, for years. I have taught everything from elementary school students to senior centers. But at a nursing home? This would be a new experience.

"Well, what do you have in mind?" I asked, trying to conceal the sleep still thick in my voice.

"Dr. Giles has been a resident here for several years and I think you know him. His son said that you might come do that for us one afternoon."

Dr. Giles has been a friend of mine for a long time and had been diagnosed with Alzheimer's. In the past, we've shared the love of shagging and listening to beach music.

"Yes, I'd love to," I answered her. "What day and time would work best for you?"

We set up an afternoon for the adventure, and I invited several friends of mine who love to shag to join me in putting on a program that the residents would enjoy. I had a boom box and some CD's under my arm as we walked in to see about 25 men and women lined around the room. Some had walkers and others were in wheel chairs. Most had blank looks and sad, lonely eyes. Dr. Giles grinned from ear to ear when he recognized me.

"Hey, Kae, are we going to shag today?"

"Absolutely. We'll show them how it's done, Frank!"

After a few minutes of talking about the Shag and its history, I turned on the music. My friends and I danced one song and then asked if some of them wanted to try. Dr. Giles got up and along with several of my friends started to cut a rug. The residents loved it. Soon they were tapping their feet and clapping their hands, with beautiful smiles and laughing eyes.

Finally, I asked, "Before we go, is there anyone else who wants to dance but hasn't?

A heavy-set lady who was sitting in her wheel chair raised her hand. It took three of us to pull her up, but once we did, we held onto her and she swayed back and forth to the song, Carolina Girl. She was laughing and having the time of her life. She was once again a "Carolina Girl" if just for a few minutes. Everyone clapped as we eased her back down into her chair.

Our time was up. We told them all goodbye, giving them big hugs before we left, and assured them we would be back.

As my friends and I were leaving, we asked each other who was more blessed, them or us? We all agreed that we were the most blessed. Thank you, Lord for giving us the health and desire to brighten their day. And thank you for giving us those residents to brighten ours.

Jim

The steps of a good man are ordered by the Lord
and He delights in his way."
Psalms 37:23

When I was a child, my family lived in Greenville, South Carolina. Fifty years ago, we moved away. Ironically, ten years ago, both of my children moved to Greenville and are raising their families there. Even though I live on the Isle of Palms outside of Charleston, I purchased a condo in Greenville there for myself to spend half of each week near them and be part of their lives.

Now that I was living in Greenville part of the week, I was able to accept a position at Furman University (which is located in Greenville) to teach dancing part time. A nice older man named Jim signed up for several of my courses and seemed to thoroughly enjoy them. He was happily married to a beautiful lady who preferred to spend her extra time taking classes of other kinds.

One night he asked me "Do you think you could come teach Shag dancing at my church some time?"

"Which church is that?" I asked.

"First Baptist of Greenville."

First Baptist was the same church my family attended fifty years ago when I was a little girl. Like most Baptist churches at that time, it did not approve of dancing. "I grew up in that church," I told him. "Do you really think they're ready for dance lessons?"

"Well, I'm the Chairman of the Deacons, and I think we can make that happen," he said with a smile.

Sure enough, not long after, the church approved of my teaching classes there. To my surprise, I received a call from a committee asking if I·would consider leading a dance program to kick off the fall season. I was thrilled! After much planning and many practices, we had over three hundred children, teenagers, and adults moving to the music. The theme was "Dance into Fall." Only God could make this happen. Never in my wildest dreams did I think I would see the members of the church of my youth not only approve of, but enjoying, dancing!

Unfortunately, the night of the program, Jim was in the hospital fighting cancer and unable to attend the program for which he was the inspiration. It was hard for me to hold back tears when they introduced me to the crowd and I then announced to them, "This night is dedicated to my special friend, Jim, who is fully responsible for my being here. Thank you, Jim."

And, thank you, Lord for putting such wonderful people in my life.

Dancing For Dollars

Let them give thanks to the Lord…
Psalm 107:8

I never thought about being a grandmother early in my life, and now it's my most favorite role. When any of my four grand-daughters say, "Mama Kae…" I am ready to reply, "Yes, dear? Do you want my car? My house? Whatever you want, it's yours!"

The Carolina Shag Club in Greenville, South Carolina, where my family and I live, host a gathering each year called "Meet Me in the Middle." About four hundred dancers come for the weekend to visit and shag. An important part of the first evening is an event called "Dancing for Dollars," which is a time for the Junior Shaggers to dance and raise money for a good cause. All four of my granddaughters were invited to participate, but only three were available this particular night.

We all love to stay together in a hotel on special occasions and this weekend is one of those fun occasions. This particular night we were staying at the Hilton, the same hotel that was holding the event. Before their dance was scheduled to begin, each of my granddaughters excitedly put on her dress for the dance, brushed her hair, and put in last minute bows.

We made it to the ballroom just in time to be introduced and the girls dashed out as the lights flashed onto the dancers. True to the name of the dance, people began showering the dancers with dollar bills and continued throughout the entire song until the bills covered the ballroom floor. When the dance was over, the dancers scooped up the money. Thousands of dollars were collected that night benefiting the needs of Junior Shaggers across the country. The donations cover expenses such as dance shoes, travel costs, and lessons.

After the dance, the girls and I headed back to our room, laughing and talking, ready for a good night's sleep. Soon after saying our prayers, giving each other good night kisses, tired but exhilarated, we all called out to each other,

"Good night, Brooke!"

"Good night, Pressley Ann!"

"Good night, Tate. Sleep tight."

"Good night, Mama Kae," they all said in unison.

Thank you, Lord, for your love. And for grandchildren. And for teaching us the joy we can receive from helping others.

I Don't Have To Come Back

He heals all my diseases.
Psalm 103:3

What did she say? I don't have to come back? Ever?

"Only if you have any concerns do you need to come back. Everything has checked out well, and it's been five years. You're doing wonderfully!"

It was my normal six-month check up with my oncologist who I had been seeing for five years. I remember the routine visit I'd had after two years. Since I had always heard that two years was a big milestone for cancer survivors. I smiled and said to her, "It's been two years."

"Yes," she said smiling back, "but five years will be even better."

My excitement quickly faded. "So will I still need to come every six months?"

"Yes."

"For how long?"

"Probably forever. Once you have had anal cancer, your chances of having another tumor are pretty high and there are several things that I want to keep an eye on."

But, now I had reached the five year milestone, and my doctor was saying this:

"Everything looks so perfect, I see no need for you to come back to me on a regular basis."

"And the lump on my leg?" I asked.

My regular doctor had been concerned about a small lump on my leg that he had seen two weeks prior. I had wondered, *Will I never be able to dance again?*

"No, that is nothing to worry about. Just a little fatty tissue. I will send him a note to that effect."

I couldn't believe it. I was in a daze.

I hugged her and walked out into the same waiting room that I was so familiar with as a patient being treated. My mind flashed back to those chemo and radiation visits I had gone through for months. The nausea and weakness I remembered so vividly. My daughter or son pushing me in a wheel chair for those last visits....and it's over? I walked over to say goodbye to a lady whom I had just met while waiting on my blood work and sat down beside her. Even though we had only just met that day, I felt close to her. There is an immediate bond between you and someone else who is going through what you are experiencing. No matter how hard I tried I could not hold back the tears of joy as I looked at her empathetic face. She took my hand and said, "I am so happy for you." She understood.

As I walked out of that cold building, the sun was warmer, the breeze was nicer and the birds were singing just a little more sweetly. I sat down on the bench that had been placed beside a beautiful shade tree in honor of Susan Komen. While I sat there praising God for this healing, one Bible verse kept coming to my mind: Psalm 103:2-3. "Praise the Lord," I told myself, "and never forget the good things He does for me… He heals all my diseases."

"Thank you, Lord," I said as I reached for my phone to call my family and friends to tell them the good news.

I am cancer free and the dance will go on!

One Last Dance

*He will wipe away every tear from their eyes,
and death shall be no more, neither shall there
be mourning, nor crying, nor pain anymore,
for the former things have passed away.*
Revelation 21:4

I guess it's like one last round of golf for the golf enthusiast; or one last tennis match at the end of a beautiful day for the avid tennis player. The bridge player wants just one more good hand before the game ends. That's the way it was for Henry, a friend of mine of thirty-five years. He wanted one last dance.

Henry was a big man, at least 6'3" tall. We'd enjoyed being neighbors for many years, and we both loved shag dancing. As he got older and suffered some health issues, Henry had become confined to a wheel chair, sadly putting his shagging days behind him. His wife had her own health issues and was diagnosed with Parkinson's disease. Due to his physical limitations, Henry was unable to care for her. Together, they moved into the Sands Nursing Home to get the care they needed. Since I was already making regular visits to the home to see another friend, I was happy to be able to keep up with Henry. Eventually, his wife passed away.

Over the following months, I continued my visits to the home. Knowing I was a dance teacher, the Activities Director asked on several different occasions if I could gather some dance friends and come to the home to demonstrate the Shag. I was always more than happy to comply with her request. What fun it was to see the joy on their faces! Though many of the residents were confined to wheelchairs, all enjoyed watching and listening to the beach music we'd brought with us.

On one of those shag visits, just before my friends and I left, I asked the crowd, "Does anybody else want to shag before we go?"

"I want to shag with you," someone called to me from the back of the room. I looked around and there was Henry grinning from ear to ear.

It took three of us to pull him to his feet from his wheel chair. He was stooped over and wobbly, but he firmly held my hand and began swaying to the music. It was just his upper body, since he couldn't move his legs.

But what a smile on my dear friend's face!

When the music ended, we quickly slid him back into his wheel chair before he could fall.

"Thank you Kae. That was great!" he said.

The next week I got the sad call that Henry had passed away peacefully in his sleep. I had the opportunity to say a few words at his memorial service and ended with "Save me a dance, Henry, I'll be there with you before we know it."

Thank you, Lord, for giving us a passion to enjoy life here on earth, thank you for Henry's one last dance, and thank you for the knowledge that one day we will be altogether in Heaven with you.

And, yes, you guessed it, I think we may even be dancing the Shag!

Henry's last dance.

They Are Perfect

As for God, His way is perfect.
Psalm 18:30

I teach a course at the University of South Carolina called "Shag Dance." Throughout the course, I allow the students to dance in their socks if they don't have loafers or shoes with leather bottom soles. On one evening each semester, I take them to shag with members of my local shag club: The Carolina Shag Club. But on this occasion they can't wear socks!

The day before our planned dancing event, I received a text from a student named Robert. We all know students are on a tight budget. He asked me "Any suggestions as to where I can buy a pair of cheap loafers?"

"What size?"

"Twelve or twelve-and-a-half."

That night, I happened to be going out to shag with some of the members of my club. I walked in through a different door than is usual for me and ran into two couples I've known for years.

Without even thinking, I asked one of the men named Alton, "Do y'all happen to know of anyone who might wear a size twelve or twelve-and-a-half shoe and have an old pair of dance shoes they can spare for a student of mine? I'm taking them out dancing tomorrow night."

"Yes, I do," Alton said.

"Really?"

"Yep. Can you come by my house tomorrow and pick them up?"

"That's incredible! What time can I come by?"

Once I had them in my hand the next day, I began the drive to Columbia to take my students dancing.

"And who says He doesn't watch over us?" I mused to myself as I drove along. "Little miracles. Now I just hoped they would fit."

I had arranged to meet the students at the door of the club where we would be dancing. There was Robert standing expectantly with the other students. We all watched as he sat down and tried the dancing shoes on. "Perfect," he said. The shoes fit him like a glove.

My friend's old shoes helped to keep Robert moving all over the dance floor that night. I don't know who was grinning more – him or me.

"Thank you, Lord," I said to myself.

Robert's dancing shoes.

Father Daughter Dance

*I have come that they may have life and that
they may have it more abundantly.*
John 10:11

The way we learn to love our earthly father often affects the way we learn to love our heavenly Father.

Some little girls do not have the advantage of growing up with an earthly father who lavishes as much attention on them as my son, Brad, does on his daughters. He has two little girls who adore him and he adores them.

One time, when my granddaughters were four and six, a father-daughter dance was coming up. They were so excited. Brad often travels but had made sure to be in town for this occasion. He had dressed in a suit and tie, ordered flowers for them, and arranged to have a limousine pick them up. He wanted this night to be perfect and for them to feel cherished.

When the night finally arrived, the girls took turns dancing with their daddy and enjoyed eating all the delicious treats. On the way home at the end of the evening, they both fell asleep, one on each of Brad's shoulders, right after whispering "I love you, Daddy."

The story of that night reminds me how much God, our Father in Heaven, cherishes each of us; even more than my son cherishes his daughters. Every day He lavishes his love upon us, so that we may have life more abundantly and a hope for eternity. The Bible, His love letter to us, tells us so. This Father, our heavenly Father, deserves to be called Daddy so we can gratefully say to Him, "I love you, Daddy."

Kae's son Brad, and granddaughters Brooke and Pressley Ann.

Let's Dance, Mama Kae!

For just as the heavens are higher than the earth,
so are my ways higher than yours, and my thoughts than yours.
Isaiah 55:9

It was spring break for my granddaughters and I was hoping to spend some time with them. After checking with them, all four seemed to be busy the entire week. I was feeling neglected and almost teary. We all used to be so close, but they are growing up so quickly and now their lives are filled with their own activities.

Then, one day that week, my phone rang. It was my oldest granddaughter, fifteen-year-old Addie. She asked, "What are you doing today, Mama Kae?"

"I don't really have anything to do today. Why?"

"Well, you do now! Let's go downtown," she said.

I couldn't get dressed quickly enough. I picked her up and we headed to a beautiful park in the middle of our town. As we got out of the car, her hand reached out to hold mine. We walked, swinging our arms, down the path beside the river. She has a way of making me feel fifteen again. What a great feeling!

Right in the middle of the path, she stopped and said, "Let's dance, Mama Kae."

I was thrilled.

She loves to shag almost as much as I do. We held hands and practiced every step I had ever taught her.

She said, "Let's do a double turn."

Then, "Let's do a pivot."

Then, "Let's do the sugar foot."

After a while, we looked up the hill and there were several people eating dinner at an outdoor restaurant. They were watching us dance and smiling down at us. We smiled back, giggling. Holding each other's hand, we ran away down the path.

It made me think about the plaque my daughter has hanging in her home. It reads, "Enjoy the little things, because one day you may look back and realize that they were really the big things."

For me, life doesn't get much bigger than this.

I've Missed You

Show me Thy ways, Oh, Lord; teach me Thy path.
Psalms 25:4

My home for the past twenty-five years has been on the Isle of Palms, outside Charleston, South Carolina. I live alone now that I am a widow, and my children live out of town. Among other things, this means that I have a lot of time to spend with the Lord. Every morning I have several devotional books that I love to linger over. *Jesus Calling*, by Sarah Young, *Streams in the Desert*, by L.B. Cowman and Jim Reimann, and *Breaking Free*, by Beth Moore, are my favorites.

I have seldom had visits from both my son's and daughter's families at the same time. But when all of the children are around I am up early in the morning because one of my four granddaughters has peeked into my bedroom to see if I'm awake. From then on it's go, go, go, until bedtime. There is no time alone for devotionals.

One time, after one of these family visits, all of my company had left for home, and I was exhausted. I had planned a trip to Myrtle Beach the next day for a dancing convention with two girlfriends. I almost canceled the trip because I was too tired, but I decided to go anyway. Due to a series of unforeseen events, both of my girlfriends had last minute conflicts and couldn't come until the second night. I found myself alone for the first night.

Our room was ocean-front. When I woke up that morning, I opened the door to the balcony and stepped out. I heard the waves breaking on the shore and smelled the salt in the air. I had a steaming cup of coffee in my hand and was ready to "do" my devotional. Suddenly, I was overwhelmed. Tears flowed from my eyes and it was as if I heard Jesus say, "I've missed you." I couldn't stop crying as I felt warm arms around me and heard Him telling me how much He loved me. His presence was so real and I realized how much I had missed Him, too. He loves us. Even though we sometimes forget or just don't take the time to love Him back, He loves us.

Forgive me, Lord, for I'm the one who missed out on the blessing and your guidance in showing me your ways. Thank you for being such a loving Father.

He Loves To Dance

Let them praise his name with dancing and make
music to him with timbrel and harp.
Psalm 149:3

Certainly, the most rewarding thing about teaching dance is the people I meet. A recently-retired man was referred to me for Shag lessons when he moved into town. He said he felt like he could shag when he was in college but later realized it was that he was under the influence of alcohol and realized he only "thought" he could shag. He has not been drinking now for many years and learning to be a good shagger is on his bucket list.

We arranged for him to have a lesson every day that I was in town which was usually three days a week. I had never known anyone as determined to learn as he was. He had never been married or had children but had spent most of his adult life working. Now he had the time and resources to pursue shag dancing.

Three months had passed since he began lessons and he was slowly becoming a confident dancer. During those lessons we had such interesting conversations about life and our many experiences living it. He told me he had become close to the Lord and was active in his church. On several occasions he brought Christian magazines and booklets to the lesson to share.

Many friends of mine were surprised at how much time we were spending together. "Maybe it's YOU he's interested in, not the Shag," they speculated.

But I assured them, "No, he's just learning to love to dance!"

He had progressed to being able to dance with my weekly group lessons and had lost all fear. I would catch him with a smile where a frown used to be as he moved with his partner across the floor.

When I observe him dancing all this time later, I feel as proud as a mother watching her child when I see all the fun he is having now that he's learned to dance.

Lord, thank you for the joy we can find in dancing.

Spencer

*Do not be anxious about anything, but in
everything by prayer and petition, with thanksgiving,
present your request to God.*
Philippians 4:6

Who can I get to help me demonstrate the Shag?

I had been hired to teach the Shag to a group of about two hundred conference attendees on Hilton Head Island, South Carolina. I love doing this sort of thing. It's wonderful to meet new people and watch how, after just a couple of hours, people who never thought they could dance begin euphorically spinning around the floor.

Usually I teach alone, but the contract for this party stipulated that I have a partner. My friend, Pete, had planned to be my partner. Unfortunately, his back began giving him trouble several days before the event. My mind raced as I tried to think of every possible solution to replace Pete, but no one I thought of could be there. I considered praying about my predicament, but I thought it may be too small a thing to worry God with. Yet, I reasoned, doesn't the Bible say that He cares about our every need? Well, I believe He does. So, I prayed: Lord, please answer my prayer and take care of this problem!

The night arrived and the event had been set up outside by the ocean. It was a gorgeous evening! One hundred and fifty people were there and, to my surprise, there were a lot of children. I decided to start with a line dance. A line dance requires no partner and is easy for children to learn. When I asked for volunteers to come up to the front, I had ten or so, mostly boys and girls. They listened intently while I reviewed the steps of the *Electric Slide*. Some caught on quickly and were soon confidently moving to the music. Among the children dancing, was a precious little boy who later tells me, using his fingers to show me, that he is three years old. His name was Spencer.

After I taught the crowd several more line dances, I asked how many would like to learn to do the Shag. To encourage participation, I told them all you need to be able to do is to count to six and know your right from your left. A large group of volunteers poured to the front, and Spencer stood right beside me with those big brown eyes watching my every move. Eventually Spencer's parents, who had been sitting at a table nearby, asked him if he would like to go back to their table. He took my hand, shook his head and said, "No, not yet." My heart melted. I've never wanted to take a little child home with me more. I laughed to myself and thought: God has sent my partner! He certainly has a sense of humor, doesn't He?

We spent the rest of evening dancing by the ocean with the beautiful hotel in the background. At the end, the woman in charge said to me, "It was all about the children tonight and everyone loved it!"

I went to bed that night smiling at the thought of how good our God is. All we need to do is put our worries in His hands.

Thank you, Lord.

David Danced

And David danced before the Lord with all his might.
2 Sam 6:14

The worship leader danced around the stage as the praise team led our time of worship. She didn't seem to have planned it, but she just couldn't be still. The music moved her to joyfully dance before the Lord. Watching her, moved me.

To dance with such joy is a beautiful way to express our love for God. The Bible tells us of many people who danced in those times, but the one I visualize more than anyone else is David. Can you imagine what it must have looked like for such an influential man to be dancing down the street unashamedly? I'm sure there were those watching who did not approve or like it. You can almost hear the crowd whispering to each other:

"What does he think he's doing?"

"What could make a grown man do such a crazy thing?"

"Has he no shame?"

These might have been the comments from onlookers that day.

Unfortunately, to this day, dancing is still sometimes criticized. I'm the first to admit that there may be good reason for that. Some so-called "dance moves" are not done in the best of taste. I grew up in a church that did not encourage or approve of dancing, but my friends and family would often dance when we were together. Thankfully now, that church of my youth, has opened its mind and doors to dancing and sees it as a healthy, wholesome activity.

Even though I can't see myself getting up on the stage in church and dancing before thousands of people, I'm happy I can appreciate that girl's enthusiasm. My prayer is for others to experience the joy of worshiping the Lord with such freedom.

A Tribute To Clint

*I press on to reach the end of the race and
receive the heavenly prize for which God,
through Christ Jesus, is calling us.*
Philippians 3:14

Shag clubs are made up of people who enjoy Shag dancing, listening to beach music, or just getting together with friends. A wonderful man named Clint passed away, and at the funeral several people from the Charleston Shag Club spoke briefly about his life. I wrote a poem and read it from the pulpit. It went like this:

I got the call from Lisa this morning.
And I wasn't prepared for what she had to say.
I had hoped that it was for some other reason;
But she had called to tell me that Clint had passed away.

My mind went back to when we first met;
It was on the dance floor, you bet.

He was one of the best partners I've ever had;
Always so good – never bad.

Knowing this sweet, sweet man was such a pleasure.
We all recognized that he was a treasure.
On the dance floor he could move those feet.
And time spent with Clint was always a treat.

His sister, Patty, was already a neighbor of mine.
And such a close family they were.
She was always talking about her brother.
And for years she and Clint took care of their mother.

When Clint started mentioning Lisa, his special friend,
We had no idea that she would be his mate until the end.
Such a happy couple – their love was clear,
That this one would work for many a year.

We were all saddened to hear of Clint's disease,
Could there not be some help for him, please??
No more dancing or doing some of the things he loved to do;
But his courage and faith in God always remained true.

Like I said, the call I got from Lisa today.
Caused me to immediately pray.
That one day we'll all be together and not by chance,
I'll look up and see Clint saying, "Can I have this dance?"

The Most Beautiful Dance

I am leading you step by step through your life.
Hold my hand in trusting dependence
letting me guide you through this day.
Psalm 32:8

If the dance we're performing requires a partner, we must hold our partner's hand tightly so that when he pulls us back, turns us, and draws us near again, we can follow closely. If we loosen our hold or look around, not keeping our eyes trained on Him, we'll make a mistake. The key to a beautiful dance is two moving as one.

Some of us are strong-willed. We want to lead our partner instead of following. It's a common issue dancers face. Two competing leaders can make a mess of a dance if one doesn't learn to submit.

When we commit to partner with God, we hold tightly to His hand, we keep our eyes fixed on him, and when we follow His lead, our lives become like a beautiful dance. He will show us the next step forward and the one after that. He turns us gently, then pulls us in to Him again. He is the ultimate leader, the best dance partner. Our lives are in His capable hands.

The advice I give my dance students is just as important in life - relax and enjoy the dance. Trust Him to open up the way before us as we go. And remember, just like dancing, learning to follow God takes practice. The more time we spend with Him, the better we get at it.

Whenever we get the chance, let's dance.

Some Final Thoughts

Thank you for taking the time to read this book. I hope you experienced even a small piece of the love and joy I felt writing down these precious memories. Though my life has changed so much over the years, one thing that hasn't changed is my assurance that the Lord's hand was gently guiding me. He has been right there for me during my school years, my marriage, my years raising children, and my years of counseling.

In addition to watching the dancing on the pier, I spent many hours growing up dancing around the house with my mother, father, and three sisters. Our family's tradition of dancing in our house carried over into my own home during my children's growing up years. It was not unusual for one of us to take another's hand and just start moving around to the music.

My life now is filled with teaching dance and spending time with my friends, church, children, and four granddaughters. Dancing is still a part of our family life. And God has blessed us all in every way. He constantly amazes me at how much He loves us and guides us. He loves you just as much as He loves me.

The Bible says: "Therefore everyone who hears these words of mine and puts them into practice is like a wise man who built his house on the rock. The rain came down, the streams rose, and the winds blew and beat against that house; yet it did not fall, because it had its foundation on the rock." (Matt. 7:24-25)

If I could make sure each and every person who reads this book leaves with just one thought it would be this: If we let Jesus direct our steps, we are set free to enjoy all that He has prepared for us to enjoy each and every day. He is the best leader.

If you don't know my Savior, He's waiting for you to turn to Him. You can bow your head right now and ask Him for forgiveness for your sins. Ask Him to come into your heart and fill you with His Spirit. His word says: "Believe on the Lord Jesus Christ and you will be saved." (Acts 16:31)

Psalm 95:1-2 says, "Come, let us sing for joy to the Lord; let us shout aloud to the Rock of our salvation. Let us come before Him with thanksgiving and extol Him with music and song." And, if I may be so bold to add – dance!

He loves you and so do I. I would love to hear from you about the ways God is working in your life, so please email me at kaeharperchilds@gmail.com.

And remember, life is a dance – just let Him lead.

About the Author

Kae Harper Childs grew up in Spartanburg, Greenville and Columbia, South Carolina. She received a B.S. in Business Administration from the University of South Carolina, a M. Ed. with a major in Guidance and Counseling from Clemson University, and she retired as a counselor for  Charleston County Schools. She has taught exercise, line dancing and Shag dancing in Greenwood, Hilton Head, Columbia, Greenville and Charleston.

She is presently teaching for the Town of Mount Pleasant, The University of South Carolina in Columbia, and the First Baptist Church in Greenville.

Although she has always enjoyed writing poetry for special occasions for friends and family, her writing career began with a writer's course at Furman University where she was teaching Shag classes. She gives the major credit for her growth in writing to the two ladies who started the writer's guild of which she is a member: Edie Melson and Vonnie Skelton. She is grateful for their time, effort and encouragement. She also credits Betts Keating and Jennifer Tubbiolo for bringing this project to life. She hopes in the future to write several more books including one about her granddaughters, and possibly one about her battle with cancer.

She was married to her childhood sweetheart, Don Childs, for thirty one years before he passed away in 1994. Her days are full and she's happiest when she's busy shagging, teaching, or spending time with family and friends. She's an active member of Seacoast Church in Mt. Pleasant, and a Watchcare member of First Baptist Church, Greenville. She is a speaker for Stonecroft Ministries, a worldwide Christian organization.

She has lived in Wild Dunes, outside of Charleston, for thirty five years and also owns a condo in Greenville. Kae's email address is: **kaeharperchilds@gmail.com**.

Made in the USA
Charleston, SC
10 November 2015